The Essential Jay Macpherson

The Essential
Jay Macpherson

selected by Melissa Dalgleish

The Porcupine's Quill

Library and Archives Canada Cataloguing in Publication

Macpherson, Jay, 1931–2012
[Poems. Selections]
    The essential Jay Macpherson / selected by Melissa Dalgleish.

(Essential poets ; 15)
Includes bibliographical references.
ISBN 978-0-88984-401-8 (softcover)

    I. Dalgleish, Melissa, 1982 –, editor II. Title. III. Series: Essential
poets (Erin, Ont.) ; 15

PS8525.P44A6 2017   C811'.54   C2016-907592-3

1   2   3   •   19   18   17

Published by The Porcupine's Quill, 68 Main Street, PO Box 160,
Erin, Ontario NOB ITO. http://porcupinesquill.ca

Thanks to Peter Reiner of the Macpherson Estate for permission to print
the unpublished poems and those poems which originally appeared in
Descant and Poetry. We also acknowledge Oxford University Press for
reprint permissions: Macpherson, Jay, Poems Twice Told © 1981.

Represented in Canada by Canadian Manda.
Trade orders are available from University of Toronto Press.

We acknowledge the support of the Ontario Arts Council and the Canada
Council for the Arts for our publishing program. The financial support of
the Government of Canada through the Canada Book Fund is also
gratefully acknowledged.

Table of Contents

Foreword

Jay Macpherson (1931–2012) occupies a complex and often contradictory position in Canadian poetry, one that makes her inclusion in the Essential Poets series both unquestionably necessary and yet less than obvious. Her career as a poet and as an academic is likewise full of contradictions, polarities and oppositions that both reflect and are in some ways produced by her interests in mirrors and reflections, innocence and experience, the fallen and the exalted, the excluded and the identified.

She was hailed in the 1950s as the poet Canada had been waiting for, but by the 1980s she was lamenting to Beryl Graves—wife of English poet and theorist Robert Graves, who published Macpherson's first collection (the last volume produced by his Seizin Press) as a twenty-first birthday present—that she and the other members of her poetic circle had become institutions by thirty-five and forgotten at forty-five. When Macpherson was inspired by her muses to write, for she always considered herself a muse poet, she was prolific and poems came easily; she spoke of her poems as tunes that went around in her head that she would, when they were ready, put down on paper, and she almost never revised. But when her muses abandoned her, as they did at intervals, she went silent for months or, as in her long silence between *The Boatman* and *Welcoming Disaster*, decades.

The Boatman won the Governor General's Award in 1958, was reviewed by *Poetry*, *Chatelaine* and *Time*, and became essential reading for a wide and varied audience. But Macpherson's highly allusive, enduringly formal, mostly mythopoeic work is just as often criticized for being private, obscure or impenetrable, and she is arguably better known abroad than she is at home. She was a leading figure in the Canadian mythopoeic modernist movement of the 1950s and 1960s—one that also included James Reaney, Daryl Hine, Anne Wilkinson, Eli Mandel, D.G. Jones, Douglas LePan, George Johnston, and later Margaret Atwood, Richard Outram and Gwendolyn MacEwen—and she became a new kind of literary celebrity when *The Boatman* was published. But Reaney's essay on her mythopoeic poetics, 'The Third Eye: Jay Macpherson's *The Boatman*' (1960), was the only one on her work for nearly twenty years; Reaney, Hine, Wilkinson and Johnston all had Essential Poets volumes before she did; and most of the critical attention paid to her work has focused on her later, self-published collection, *Welcoming Disaster*.

The Boatman was published in three successive editions by Oxford University Press, a commitment to Macpherson's work that kept it in print for more than forty years, but this is the first new edition of her poetry in more than thirty. Macpherson and her fellow mythopoets have been accused of writing disconnected, antiseptic, academic literature about literature instead of literature about life, but she spent the latter half of her career writing political, activist poetry rooted in the world around her. As with her verse, there is nothing simple or straightforward about Jay Macpherson's poetic career and place within Canadian letters.

The contradictions and complexities that characterize Macpherson's poetic career, one that began with the pseudonymous publication of 'Non-Identification' in the April 1947 issue of *Canadian Forum* when she was fifteen and ended only with her death in March 2012 at the age of eighty, reflect the contradictions and complexities inherent in her extraordinarily accomplished, funny, erudite, ironic, musical, and fundamentally ethical verse. Macpherson began writing verse as a child living in Newfoundland, where she had been placed in foster care after coming to Canada as a 'war guest' with her mother and brother. Alongside her *Oxford Book of English Verse*, books of myths and legends and BBC poetry broadcasts, writing was her best connection to home and to the broad community of literary people to which she already felt she belonged.

That drive for community and connection underpins not only much of Macpherson's verse, but also her work within the Canadian literary community. Macpherson turned, from the time she began writing and publishing as a teenager, to myths and legends — both biblical and classical, and later, in *Welcoming Disaster*, Sumerian — as a vocabulary that could be universally intelligible, that tapped into the shared archetypes that make up Jung's 'collective unconscious', that could bring readers into a community contained between the covers of her texts. But Macpherson was also concerned with those who were left outside that community, unidentified and unloved: the poor children, the 'fallen women', those who could not use literature as a mirror because they were not reflected in it. The cover image of this volume—a narcissus from Redouté's *Les liliacées*—reflects Macpherson's interest in mirrors and reflections, one that began as a childhood obsession with Milton's *Lycidas* and its echoes of the Narcissus myth, and continued throughout her poetic and academic career. Both her master's thesis and dissertation, published by Yale University Press as *Spirit of Solitude: Conventions and Continuities in Late Romance* (1982), are intensely concerned with the resonances of the Narcissus myth throughout literature. In *Four Ages of Man* (1964) and *Biblical and Classical Myths: The Mythological Framework of Western Culture* (which she co-authored with Northrop Frye in 2004), Macpherson worked to provide new generations of students and readers with what she believed was a crucial ability to identify mythic reflections and resonances. Macpherson herself was drawn to muses in whom she saw her own interests mirrored: P. K. Page, Alan Crawley, Grete Wels-Schön (an archetypal theorist who inspired most of Macpherson's work before 1952), Robert Graves and, most famously, Frye.

In an effort to create more opportunities for other writers to see the resonances of their work reflected back to them through the eyes of their readers, Macpherson founded Emblem Books, which published volumes by Dorothy Livesay, Al Purdy and others. She also acted as a distributor for small-press publications, wrote about the poetry readings at the 1955 Canadian Writers' Conference and produced the recording *Six Toronto Poets*. At the same time she taught and mentored generations of poets and students that included Margaret Atwood, among many others. Far from being the solitary, minor poet she sometimes described herself as, Jay Macpherson was central to the development of Canadian poetry at mid-century and onwards.

The selection of poems in this volume is intended to open new windows onto Macpherson's poetics, which were far more varied in form and content than many have realized. Macpherson has long been understood as a poet intensely concerned with structure and sequence—as Milton Wilson notes, *The Boatman* is 'the most intricately unified book in Canadian poetry'—but that is only partially true. While *The Boatman* is typically read as having been designed to resemble a full mythic cycle from innocence to fall to redemption, Margaret Atwood reminds us that her friend 'is not a programmatic writer, and her work, when it falls into sequences, does so because her imagination is working with a certain body of material, not because she thinks she needs a poem of a certain kind to fill a gap and then composes it.' *The Boatman*, rather than having been designed as a structured, apocalyptic cycle, is more properly a collected-poems edition, gathering as it does most of Macpherson's poetic production from the late 1940s until 1956, bringing together poems she published in *Contemporary Verse* (1949–1950); her first collection, *Nineteen Poems* (1952); her first Emblem Book, *O Earth Return* (1954) and its shadow side, *The Plowman in Darkness* (1955); the interlinked chapbook suites *The Shepherd by Moonlight* (1956) and *The Mind That Ocean: A Book of Riddles* (1956); the Ark suite she published in *Poetry* (1956); and a very few poems intended to flesh out *The Boatman* written in 1956.

Given that Macpherson's poems of the 1940s and 1950s have long been read within the unifying frame of *The Boatman*, and are seen as having been strongly influenced by her studies under Northrop Frye from 1953 onward, this collection seeks to detach her work from that frame and place it back within its original contexts of composition and publication. Poems are organized according to their original date and venue of publication, and selected to suggest the individual character of the suites in which they were originally published. Given that Macpherson's interest in structure and sequence was far more nuanced than she has generally been given credit for, such an approach opens up new interpretive possibilities for her verse.

The nature of Macpherson's publication history has also elided the fact that the 'other poems' published in *The Boatman and Other Poems* (1968) were written circa 1956, and Macpherson's poetic silence appears to have extended from then until the early 1970s. William Toye of Oxford University Press maintained an enduring interest in her work, and she wrote to him in 1972 to note that she had begun writing again. These poems and the many that followed became *Welcoming Disaster*, which she self-published in 1974 and which Toye republished along with *The Boatman* as *Poems Twice Told* (1981). But although that volume was Macpherson's last book of poetry, and she began to refuse to be known as a poet, she did not stop writing or publishing verse. *Poetry* magazine was a loyal supporter, as were smaller magazines like *Descant*, and Macpherson's political and activist writing circulated privately and on the University of Toronto campus via publications like *The Varsity*. This edition highlights some of that little-read later work in order to open up new avenues for exploring the development of Macpherson's poetics, and her politics, after the publication of her major collections. An even fuller understanding will be possible when the collection, assessment and (hopefully) publication of her late poems, which is under way, has been completed.

Macpherson always claimed an allegiance to what she called 'authentic myths', those that retain emotional and psychological resonance, even in their debased mass-media and marketing forms, because they speak to the fundamental feelings, dreams and desires that make us human. It is her ability to transform those myths, to retell ancient stories in new forms that tell us something about ourselves and our place in the world, that makes Macpherson one of our essential poets.

Non-Identification

Turning from shadow to shadow, we find
Nowhere the expected revelation,
Never can establish a connection
Between eye and image, surface and hand.

Contained in crying flesh and bone,
Unenvying we lack
Water's ignorance of pain,
The old indifference of stone,
Fire's easy taut and slack
— And therefore shall be hurt again.

Ordinary People in the Last Days

My mother was taken up to heaven in a pink cloud.
She was talking to a friend on the telephone
When we saw her depart through the ceiling,
Still murmuring about bridge.

My father prophesied.
He looked out from behind his newspaper
And said, 'Johnny-Boy will win the Derby.'
The odds against were fifteen to one, and he won.

The unicorn yielded to my sweetheart.
She was giggling with some girls
When the unicorn walked carefully up to her
And laid his head in her lap.

The white bull ran away with my sister.
My father sent me to find her
But the oracle maundered on about a cow
And I came home disgruntled.

The dove descended on my brother.
He was working in the garden
When the air became too bright for comfort
And the glory of the bird scorched his roses.

A mouse ran away in my wainscot.
I study all day and pray all night.
My God, send me a sign of Thy coming
Or let me die.

My mother was taken up to heaven in a pink cloud,
My father prophesied,
The unicorn yielded to my sweetheart,
The white bull ran away with my sister,
The dove descended on my brother,
And a mouse ran away in my wainscot.

Poor Child

The child is mortal; but Poor Child
Creeps through centuries of bone
Untransient as the channelling worm,
Or water making sand of stone.
Poor child, what have they done to you?

Poor child the royal goosegirl combing
Her hair in the field: poor children too
Achilles sulking, Odysseus returned,
Philoctetes, Prufrock, and you and you.
Poor child, what have they done to you?

Go farther back: for these poor children,
Ruined from the womb, still yearn
To swing in dark or water, wanting
Not childhood's flowers but absolute return.
Poor child, what have we done?

Private Deluge

This was the Golden Age. I lived entombed
In pleasure like a bee that lies entombed
In amber. Then I lived in calm delight,
Quiet and orderly as day and night.
Then I had golden apples from the trees
Of the unserpented Hesperides.
There all the walls were holy, every stone
Cried Glory; I could never be alone
But every object turned about to see,
And with familiar looks regarded me.

The fountains of an unsuspected deep
Broke up one night as I lay safe asleep;
And when I woke, the orchard waved its crown
Of fruit and leaves from many fathoms down.
The people I had loved I saw pursue
Their sweet anterior life that once I knew.
I cried and stared and shivered, tempest-hurled
Into a chaos I must make a world.

The flood was real, but only mine.
No good arms and no dear hour
Shall ever break the water's power.
I live under an Iron winter's sign.

The Comforter

My mother's bird the blessed now drifting dove
Descended cool divine and orderly,
Folding down darkness from her godbright wings.

Lucifer falling from the courts of grace
Scattering light angelically rushed past
The sun, the moon, the gravely dancing stars.
And drew about him ever-heavying night.
I when the dove rose on her sober way
Fell in a crowd of broken images,
Dear Sun, dear Moon, grave dance! to where there comes
No darkness and no light, to common day.

The Comforted

Each night I do retrace
My heavy steps and am compelled to pass
To earlier places, but take up agen
The journey's turning skein.

The thread Night's daughters spin
Runs from birth's dark to death's, a shining line.
The snipping Fate attends its end and mine,
Ends what the two begin.

My mother gave to lead
My blind steps through the maze a daedal thread:
Who slept, who wept on Naxos long has worn
A constellated crown.

The ceaseless to and from
Hushes the cry of the devouring womb
That I wind up the journey I have come
And follow it back home.

The Third Eye

Of three eyes, I would still give two for one.
The third eye clouds: its light is nearly gone.
The two saw green, saw sky, saw people pass:
The third eye saw through order like a glass
To concentrate, refine and rarify
And make a Cosmos of miscellany.
Sight, world and all to save alive that one
Fading so fast! Ah love, its light is done.

Goddesses

(For Robert)

Tell the white lady goddesses I will be theirs,
Walk in white or scarlet as their rule declares,
Cut or bind my hair, recite with candid look
The genealogies from their holy book,

Embrace what ape or fiend they will, suffer what grief,
Suckle their familiars — and if I starve my child,
Let me good Lord not trouble to be mild,
Since all was done in perfect unbelief.

Ideas of Order

Now lift your eyes
To see the nightly patterned skies.
How did they all come there,
The Hunter & his Dog, the Virgin & the Bear?

Shall we suppose
God ranged his brilliant servants to disclose
An order in the sky
Of beasts & heroes to instruct men by?

No: but when first
He knew himself to body's darkness cursed
Man dared to think to find
In heaven the order of his constellated mind.

She

She who is fickle sea
And indifferent sky
Is that true star men flee
These dangers by.

Thus I know this of you:
You will be labyrinth, and clue.

The Ill Wind

To reply, in face of a bad season,
Pestilential cold, malignity,
To the ill wind weeping on my shoulder:
'Child, what have I to do with thee?'

Is to deny the infant head
And the voice complaining tirelessly:
'Is there room for one only under your cloak,
Mother, may I creep inside and see?
Did you not know my wicked will
When you summoned me?'

Eve in Reflection

Painful and brief the act. Eve on the barren shore
Sees every cherished feature, plumed tree, bright grass,
Fresh spring, the beasts as placid as before
Beneath the inviolable glass.

There the lost girl gone under sea
Tends her undying grove, never raising her eyes
To where on the salt shell beach in reverie
The mother of all living lies.

The beloved face is lost from sight,
Marred in a whelming tide of blood:
And Adam walks in the cold night
Wilderness, waste wood.

Sibylla

Who questions now, who offers thanks, who grieves?
No memory lingers
In the sand I run between my fingers,
In the whirling leaves.

Where is your god, Sibylla? where is he
Who came in other days
To lay his bright head on your knee
And learn the secrets of Earth's ways?

Silence: the bat-clogged cave
Lacks breath to sigh.
Sibylla, hung between earth and sky,
Sways with the wind in her pendant grave.

Eurynome

In the snake's embrace mortal she lies,
Dies, but lives to renew her torment,
Under her, rock, night her eyes.
In the wall around her was set by One
Upright, staring, to watch for morning
With bread and candle, her little son.

Love in Egypt

Love, here are thorns, and here's a wilderness
— And yet you visit me?
I have a cell, your rod —
No more to see.

A spring restores these sands,
Pouring its rocky basin full.
Love, will you drink from my hands,
Or rather from my skull?

The Marriage of Earth and Heaven

(For George)

Earth draws her breath so gently, heaven bends
On her so bright a look, I could believe
That the renewal of the world was come,
The marriage of kind Earth and splendid Heaven.

'O happy pair' — the blind man lifts his harp
Down from the peg — but wait, but check the song.
The two you praise still matchless lie apart,
Thin air drawn sharp between queen Earth and Heaven.

Though I stand and stretch my hands forever
Till my hair grows down my back and my skirt to my ankles,
I shall not hear the triumphs of their trumpets
Calling the hopeful in from all the quarters
To the marriage of kind Earth and splendid Heaven.

Yet out of parting's reach a place is kept
For great occasions, with a fat four-poster bed
And a revelling-ground and a fountain showering beer
And a fiddler fiddling fine for folly's children
To riot rings around at the famous wedding
Of quean Earth and her fancy-fellow Heaven.

The Swan

White-habited, the mystic Swan
Walks her rank cloister as the night draws down,
In sweet communion with her sister shade,
Matchless and unassayed.

The tower of ivory sways,
Gaze bends to mirrored gaze:
This perfect arc embraces all her days.
And when she comes to die
The treasures of her silence patent lie:
'I am all that is and was and shall be,
My garment may no man put by.'

Sibylla

God Phoebus was a merry lad,
Courted my mother's daughter:
Said I, 'To swim I'll be quite glad,
But keep me from the water.'

He swore he'd break my looking-glass
And dock my maiden tresses;
He told me tales of many a pass,
All of them successes.

There's other ways to catch a god
Who's feeling gay and girly
Than tickling with a fishing-rod
Among the short and curly.

I took his gift and thwarted him,
I listened to his vows, and
Though looks are gone and eyes grow dim,
I'll live to be a thousand.

I'm mercifully rid of youth,
No callers plague me ever:
I'm virtuous, I tell the truth —
And you can see I'm clever!

Eurynome

Come all old maids that are squeamish
And afraid to make mistakes,
Don't clutter your lives up with boyfriends:
The nicest girls marry snakes.

If you don't mind slime on your pillow
And caresses as gliding as ice
— Cold skin, warm heart, remember,
And besides, they keep down the mice —

If you're really serious-minded,
It's the best advice you can take:
No rumpling, no sweating, no nonsense,
Oh who would not sleep with a snake?

The Rymer

Hear the voice of the Bard!
Want to know where I've been?
Under the frost-hard
Ground with Hell's Queen,
Whom there I embraced
In the dark as she lay,
With worms defaced,
Her lips gnawed away
— What's that? Well, maybe
Not everybody's dame,
But a sharp baby
All the same.

Mary of Egypt

Little children, gather round
On this bare and stony ground,
Listen while your tired and hoary
Mother tells a bed-time story.

In a far-off former time
And a green and gentle clime,
Mamma was a lively lass,
Liked to watch the tall ships pass,
Loved to hear the sailors sing
Of sun and wind and voyaging,
Felt a wild desire to be
On the bleak and unplowed sea.
Mamma was a nice girl, mind,
Hard up, but a good sport and kind —
Well, the blessed upshot was,
Mamma worked her way across
From Egypt to the Holy Land,
And here repents, among the sand.

The Anagogic Man

Noah walks with head bent down;
For between his nape and crown
He carries, balancing with care,
A golden bubble round and rare.

Its gently shimmering sides surround
All us and our worlds, and bound
Art and life, and wit and sense,
Innocence and experience.

Forbear to startle him, lest some
Poor soul to its destruction come,
Slipped out of mind and past recall
As if it never was at all.

O you that pass, if still he seems
One absent-minded or in dreams,
Consider that your senses keep
A death far deeper than his sleep.

Angel, declare: what sways when Noah nods?
The sun, the stars, the figures of the gods.

The Secret Sleeper

His sleep sustains the golden tree,
His night the shining day,
His calm the turtle on her nest,
His rest the fountain-spray.

He need not ask for whose delight
His flowering dreams will rise,
Nor buried in what crystal breast
He securely lies.

The Garden of the Sexes

I have a garden closed away
And shadowed from the light of day
Where Love hangs bound on every tree
And I alone go free.

His sighs that turn the weathers round,
His tears that water all the ground,
His blood, that reddens in the vine,
These are all mine.

At night the golden apple-tree
Is my fixed station, whence I see
Terrible, sublime and free,
My loves go wheeling over me.

Go take the world ...

Go take the world my dearest wish
And blessing, little book.
And should one ask who's in the dish
Or how the beast was took,
Say: Wisdom is a silver fish
And Love a golden hook.

Egg

Reader, in your hand you hold
A silver case, a box of gold.
I have no door, however small,
Unless you pierce my tender wall,
And there's no skill in healing then
Shall ever make me whole again.
Show pity, Reader, for my plight:
Let be, or else consume me quite.

Phoenix

If I am that bird, then I am one alone.
Father, mother, child, I am my own.
Ashes and bone of a dead life I save
And bear about with me to find a grave,
Token that my renewed and lively breath
Is kindled from a still-repeated death.
That fire is my element, consumes and lights me,
Heals and accuses and again requites me.
I feed on the dew of heaven and live without desire:
Reader, consider a life in the fire.

Book

Dear Reader, not your fellow flesh and blood
—I cannot love like you, nor you like me—
But like yourself launched out upon the flood,
Poor vessel to endure so fierce a sea.

The water-beetle travelling dry and frail
On the stream's face is not more slight than I;
Nor more tremendous is the ancient whale
Who scans the ocean floor with horny eye.

Although by my creator's will I span
The air, the fire, the water and the land,
My volume is no burden to your hand.

I flourish in your sight and for your sake.
His servant, yet I grapple fast with man:
Grasped and devoured, I bless him. Reader, take.

Retina

The struggler in the net
His agon past
Through a true gate
Comes in at last,
Leaving behind him
In quite a fix
An old man's skin and bones
Cross as two sticks.

The Fisherman

The world was first a private park
Until the angel, after dark,
Scattered afar to wests and easts
The lovers and the friendly beasts.

And later still a home-made boat
Contained Creation set afloat,
No rift nor leak that might betray
The creatures to a hostile day.

But now beside the midnight lake
One single fisher sits awake
And casts and fights and hauls to land
A myriad forms upon the sand.

Old Adam on the naming-day
Blessed each and let it slip away:
The fisher of the fallen mind
Sees no occasion to be kind,

But on his catch proceeds to sup;
Then bends, and at one slurp sucks up
The lake and all that therein is
To slake that hungry gut of his,

Then whistling makes for home and bed
As the last morning breaks in red;
But God the Lord with patient grin
Lets down his hook and hoicks him in.

Ark Apprehensive

I am a sleeping body
Hulling down the night,
And you the dream I ferry
To shores of light.

I sleep that you may wake,
That the black sea
May not gape sheer under you
As he does for me.

Ark Overwhelmed

When the four quarters shall
Turn in and make one whole,
Then I who wall your body,
Which is to me a soul,

Shall swim circled by you
And cradled on your tide,
Who was not even, not ever,
Taken from your side.

Ark Parting

You dreamed it. From my ground
You raised that flood, these fears.
The creatures all but drowned
Fled your well of tears.

Outward the fresh shores gleam
Clear in new-washed eyes.
Fare well. From your dream
I only shall not rise.

The Love-Song of Jenny Lear

Come along, my old king of the sea,
Don't look so pathetic at me:
We're off for a walk
And a horrid long talk
By the beautiful banks of the sea.

I'm not Arnold's Margaret, the pearl
That gleamed and was lost in a whirl,
Who simpered in churches
And left him on porches,
But more of a hell of a girl.

Poor old fish, you're no walker at all,
Can't you spank up that elderly crawl?
I'll teach you to hurdle,
Led on by my girdle,
With whalebone, elastic and all.

We'll romp by the seashore, and when
You've enough, shut your eyes and count ten.
I'll crunch down your bones,
Guts marrow and stones,
Then raise you up dancing again.

Love-Song II of Jenny Lear

Were I a Shakespearean daughter,
Safe restored through fire and water,
You the party in the crown
—Someone get the curtain down.

The Beauty of Job's Daughters

The old, the mad, the blind have fairest daughters.
Take Job: the beasts the accuser sends at evening
Shoulder his house and shake it; he's not there,
Attained in age to inwardness of daughters,
In all the land no women found so fair.

Angels and sons of God are nearest neighbours,
And even the accuser may repair
To walk with Job in pleasures of his daughters:
Wide shining rooms more warmly lit at evening,
Gardens beyond whose secrets scent the air.

Not wiles of men nor envy of the neighbours,
Riches of earth, nor what heaven holds more rare,
Can take from Job the beauty of his daughters,
The gardens in the rock, music at evening,
And cup so full that all who come must share.

Perhaps we passed them? it was late, or evening,
And surely those were desert stumps, not daughters,
In fact we doubt that they were ever there.
The old, the mad, the blind have fairest daughters.
In all the land no women found so fair.

Of Creatures the Net

I
Of creatures the net and chain
Stretched like that great membrane
The soft sore ocean
Is by us not broken;

And like an eye or tongue
Is wet and sensing;
And by the ends drawn up
Will strain but not snap.

II
And in all natures we
The primitive he and she
Carry the child Jesus,
Those suffering senses

That in us see and taste,
With us in absence fast,
For whose scattered and bound
Sake we are joined.

III
Of the seas the wide cup
Shrinks to a water-drop,
The creatures in its round
As in an eye contained,

And that eye still the globe
Wherein all natures move,
Still tough the skin
That holds their troubles in.

IV
In all the green flood
More closely binds than blood;
Though windowed like a net
Lets none forget

The forsaken brother
And elder other;
Divided is unbroken,
Draws with the chain of ocean.

A Mermaid's Grave

You who would Love's wonders see,
Pity my extremity.
He, by envy moved to intend
I should make a proper end,
Smote the waters till they boiled,
Rent my person neatly coiled,
Then, of his amusement tiring,
Cast me on green ground expiring.

Now unfeeling earth's my bed,
And round the cockle borders tread
Children, singing as they go:
'Here lies the cold mermaid, alive, alive-oh.'

No Man's Nightingale

Sir, no man's nightingale, your foolish bird,
I sing and thrive, by Angel finger fed,
And when I turn to rest, an Angel's word
Exalts an air of trees above my head,
Shrouds me in secret where no single thing
May envy no-man's-nightingale her spring.

The Boatman

You might suppose it easy
For a maker not too lazy
To convert the gentle reader to an Ark:
But it takes a willing pupil
To admit both gnat and camel
— Quite an eyeful, all the crew that must embark.

After me when comes the deluge
And you're looking round for refuge
From God's anger pouring down in gush and spout,
Then you take the tender creature
— You remember, that's the reader —
And you pull him through his navel inside out.

That's to get his beasts outside him,
For they've got to come aboard him,
As the best directions have it, two by two.
When you've taken all their tickets
And you've marched them through his sockets,
Let the tempest bust Creation: heed not you.

For you're riding high and mighty
In a gale that's pushing ninety
With a solid bottom under you — that's his.
Fellow flesh affords a rampart,
And you've got along for comfort
All the world there ever shall be, was, and is.

Leviathan

Now show thy joy, frolic in Angels' sight
Like Adam's elephant in fields of light.
There lamb and lion slumber in the shade.
Splendour and innocence together laid.

The Lord that made Leviathan made thee
Not good, not great, not beautiful, not free,
Not whole in love, not able to forget
The coming war, the battle still unmet.

But look: Creation shines, as that first day
When God's Leviathan went forth to play
Delightful from his hand. The brute flesh sleeps,
And speechless mercy all that sleeping keeps.

A Dry Light

What if my bed is Egypt's clay,
I might still offer passage-way
And baffle all men know of me,
Dividing for you like a sea,
To let you march where none yet tried,
Laid up in heaps to either side.

Then safely bear your little light,
So prized, so clear, so angel-bright.
I'll threaten neither hair nor toe;
But cannot tell you where you go.
Say, Prophet, on my farther strand,
If wilderness, if promised land.

The Dark Air

Look: forests, cities, gardens, fair
Expanding in the upward air.
The same world hangs below, but dark,
Unlit by any dreaming spark,
And there the flowering world of light
Seeks its roots in deepest night.

That head you bear above the earth,
Exalted from a different birth,
Whose gardens, cities, forests, seem
Substantial and our day their dream,
Lay down, for in your night I see.
Set in my body, sleep in me.

Poets & Muses

Poets are such bad employers,
Muses ought to Organize:
Time off, sick pay, danger wages —
Come, ye wretched of the skies!

Poets, to reverse the story,
Muse-redeemed, return and live:
Solomon in all his glory
Could not pay for what you give.

P.S.
Breathing too is a simple trick, and most of us learn it:
Still, to lose it is bad, though no-one regrets it long.

Hampstead Ponds

Pools where I fished with jamjars for minnows, mysterious
Waters, linked underground, unsearchable source:
Home where I come from, well that all flow from, than memory
Deeper, the dreamland sluice that restores our friends:
Distant, sealed with a stone, but murmuring always:
If I forget thee, O secret fountain, forget not me.

Absence, Havoc

Absence, havoc — well, I missed you —
Near and dear turned far and strange,
Dayshine came disguised as midnight:
One thing altered made all change.

Fallen? stolen? trapped? entangled?
To a lower world betrayed?
Endless error held your footsteps,
On your brow a deepening shade.

Long I sought you, late I found you,
Straying on the farther shore:
You indeed? a swaying phantom
Fades, that flickered on before.
Lost, no rescue: only dreams our
Wandered, wandered loves restore.

Some Ghosts & Some Ghouls

While we loved those who never read our poems,
Answered our letters, said the simple things we
Waited so long for, and were too polite to
    See we were crying.

Irony fed us: for the days we watched our
Chances to please them, nights in ruled beds lay
Gored by their phantoms, guilty most of suffering,
    We were rewarded.

While we admired how ignorance became them,
Coldness adorned, they came at length to trust us,
Made us their mirrors: last their hopeless loves to
    Us they confided.

They were our teachers: what we are, they made us.
Cautious our converse, prudent our behaviour,
Guarded our faces: we behind them lurking,
    Greedy, devourers.

Lady Haunts Ghosts

Others there are whose phantoms nightly rouse them,
Down the dark stair drive, shrinking but accustomed,
Nightlong to search where features are confounded:
    Them must I envy.

Mine are too faint: I take the whip and urge them,
Make them descend, their squeals and wails unheeded,
Drag them like bait for lower worlds to clutch at,
    Frail, unresisting.

Back in the light I rummage, ransack them,
Breathe them and suck them, wolfish, famished, rake for
News of my lost ones, gone where gods of darkness
    Keep, unforgiving.

A Lost Soul

Some are plain lucky—we ourselves among them:
Houses with books, with gardens, all we wanted,
Work we enjoy, with colleagues we feel close to—
    Love we have, even.

True love and candid, faithful, strong as gospel,
Patient, untiring, fond when we are fretful.
Having so much, how is it that we ache for
    Those darker others?

Some days for them we could let slip the whole damn
Soft bed we've made ourselves, our friends in Heaven
Let slip away, buy back with blood our ancient
    Vampires and demons.

First loves and oldest, what names shall I call you?
Older to me than language, old as breathing,
Born with me, in this flesh: by now I know you're
    Greed, pride and envy.

Too long I've shut you out, denied acquaintance,
Favoured less barefaced vices, hoped to pass for
Reasonable, rate with those who more inclined to
    Self-hurt than murder.

You were my soul: in arrogance I banned you.
Now I recant—return, possess me, take my
Hands, bind my eyes, infallibly restore my
    Share in perdition.

Hecate Trivia

Here in a land of faultless four-leaved clovers,
Learning from books how, back before our windows,
Mirrors, your dusty forks were where uncanny
    Worlds faced each other,

We, where our fathers banished wolf and Indian,
Vainly regret their vanished sense and vigour:
Now in our cities take a last, last stand with
    Rat and with cockroach.

Goddess of crossways, three-faced, was it you my
Muse all this while? you are the last who hallows
Contents of pockets, broken dolls, dead puppies:
    Queen, garbage-eater.

Orion

Orion is the winter-king
Among heaven's bright designs.
His up is down: his height is set
In Hell, and yet he shines.

Those stars of night the fiend drew down,
That followed in his train,
At midnight stand above the town:
They glitter in their pain.

My foolstar hero, stretched at length,
The sky's pins through his head,
Basks at those fires his dreary strength
That's slanted to the dead.

Come, darkness, fill my heart and eyes:
I'll sink below the light,
And, buried with Orion, rise
To winter and to night.

Discovery

Artless fuzzwit! was it you, then
— Infant, far from reckless teens —
Laid a powder plot, and blew the
Man of glass to smithereens?

Or, did someone — nameless, faceless —
Set you on? were you beguiled?
For such plot, my grimoires tell me,
Take a feeble-minded child.

Gentle babe, with such intentions!
Now we've seen what you could do,
Lie there, fertilize my garden:
See what earth will make of you.

Though, I never meant to lose you,
Little thorn of poison tree:
Nights I lay me down beside you,
When I wake, am still with thee.

What Falada Said

All I have left from home—the horse that brought me,
Dead, flayed, its head hung up, its power of speaking
Left, like an echo—gives its daily message
    In the dark entry:

'Daughter, betrayed and drudging here in exile,
Those who let these things happen were—believe me—
Foreigners, strangers, none of those who loved you:
    Not your true mother.

She if she knew would send someone to fetch you,
Carry you home, restore the past, again her
Child, joy from pain: at least, if she could know it
    She would be sorry.'

So on my nursery floor my dolls consoled me.
No: there are four, not two: a constellation
Turning: maimed child, barbed mother—torn, rent open
    Womb, bladed baby.

For This Ointment ...

What I can, I do: my salary is always
Shared, my response to charities not grudging
(Income-tax-lessening), presence too at meetings
Not quite unheard-of—

Meantime the sufferers crowd the roads, the children,
All lost behind them, turn to us their faces—
Writing my cheque, I pause, subtract storm windows,
Fortnight in Europe.

Blood-money, Danegelt, token sacrifices—
All of us but the few, the saints, live that way.
Something besides I still hold back—for what? whom?
Not that good woman—

She had her Lord: I clutch my gift ungiven,
Selfish and sterile—so I was commanded.
Dark god or bright I wait for, him who sent me,
Known by his absence.

The Ballad of Dr. Coolie

Here's a man was born in China, he
Heard of Canada, thought he'd go and see —
Land of Bethune, snow, opportunity —
Why not have a try?

Comes to Canada, does quite brilliantly.
Talks good English, goes through U of T,
Then to Berkeley, gets his PhD —
What's next but the sky?

Welcome back to alma mater, be
Teacher, lab man, please do brilliantly.
Then they said, Hey, take it easy, we
Think you aim too high.

Good workhorses should know their places, they
Bring no blushes to colleagues' faces, they
Keep their heads down, run no races, they
Crunch hay till they die.

Pie is not for Doctor Coolie:
God gives pie to white guys duly,
He knows white guys deserve it truly:
Professorial pie.

Plants

It's sombre, looking at plants
This dying shoot in my window
Mistreated by me all winter
Puts out what it can

A Winter Night (Long After Lampman)

From where I sit I see no stars;
But yonder, where the traffic turns,
All night across the darkness burns
DEMOS FOR SALE
ELECT USED CARS

About Jay Macpherson

Jean (Jay) Macpherson was born on June 13, 1931, in London, England, to Major James Ewan Macpherson and his wife Dorothy. The Macphersons lived in Hampstead and the nearby countryside until Macpherson was nine when, with her mother and elder brother Andrew, she sailed to Canada on the SS *Baltrover* as a 'war guest'. She was deposited with a foster family in St. John's, Newfoundland, while her mother and brother travelled to Montreal. Andrew remained there with the Reid family and Dorothy continued to Ottawa, where she began her long career at the National Film Board. Both children rejoined their mother in Ottawa in 1944; James never left England.

Macpherson soon became the editor of the Glebe Collegiate Institute student newspaper *Call to Order*, for which she wrote poetry under the pseudonym Frogden Splash. She was befriended by poet and painter P.K. Page (Irwin) and *Contemporary Verse* editor Alan Crawley, and began to publish her work in literary magazines. Her first poem appeared in *Canadian Forum* in April 1947 and many followed in *Contemporary Verse*. Macpherson spent the summers of 1948 and 1949 in Quebec with the Schön family, and her work of this period was written for and about Grete Wels-Schön, an archetypal theorist, translator and anthropologist with whom Macpherson was in love.

Upon graduating from Glebe Collegiate, Macpherson pursued a B.A. in Classics at Carleton University, where she befriended Canadian poet and professor George Johnston and the German Gnostic philosopher Hans Jonas, for whom she worked as an amanuensis and translator. Macpherson pursued a year of Honours English study at University College London after gradation, and was there introduced to Robert Graves, author of *The White Goddess* (1948). She spent a month at his home in Mallorca, and he published her first collection, *Nineteen Poems* (1952), as a twenty-first-birthday present.

Macpherson then began a library sciences degree at McGill, and Johnston insisted she meet Northrop Frye on a class trip to Toronto. This meeting convinced her to enrol in graduate school at Victoria College, University of Toronto, in 1953. She published the first two editions by her own Emblem Books press in early 1955 — her *O Earth Return* and Daryl Hine's *Five Poems* — and completed her master's thesis on Milton's *Lycidas* that fall. She then continued to the Ph.D. under

Frye's supervision, one focused on the pastoral in romantic literature. She and Frye likely became romantically involved around this time.

In quick succession, Macpherson composed suites and chapbooks including *The Plowman in Darkness* (1955), *The Shepherd by Moonlight* (1956), *The Mind That Ocean: A Book of Riddles* (1956), the Ark poems (1956), *Pretty Ophelia!* (1956) and other verse published in a wide variety of Canadian and American literary magazines. She also published through Emblem Books works by Dorothy Livesay, Heather Spears and Violet Anderson and worked as a distributor for other small publishers. In early 1957, Macpherson became the first Canadian to win the *Poetry* magazine Levinson Prize for her Ark poems, and shortly thereafter her selected works were published by Oxford University Press as *The Boatman*. Macpherson became the youngest person ever to win the Governor General's Award for Poetry, and *The Boatman* was widely read and acclaimed.

After the publication of *The Boatman*, Macpherson stopped publishing verse — with the exception of *A Dry Light & The Dark Air* (1959), plus a poem and the text to John Beckwith's cantata *Jonah* in *Alphabet* — for nearly two decades. She turned her attentions to teaching (she was appointed to the faculty of Victoria College in 1957), publishing (including volumes by Al Purdy and Alden Nowlan), scholarship, writing *Four Ages of Man: The Classical Myths* (1962) and acting as poet-advisor and translator for the revision of *The Hymn Book of the Anglican Church of Canada and the United Church of Canada* (1971), a task she relished despite the fact that she was unreligious. Milton Wilson took over the supervision of her doctorate in 1960, and she completed it in 1964.

Macpherson broke her long poetic silence in the early 1970s and *Welcoming Disaster* (1974) soon followed, self-published by Saanes Publications; both her major works were collected in *Poems Twice Told* (1981). She continued to write poetry (often political), pursue research and mentor her students even after her retirement in 1996. Her dissertation was published as *Spirit of Solitude: Conventions and Continuities in Late Romance* (1982); she and Frye also co-authored *Biblical and Classical Myths: The Mythological Framework of Western Culture* (2004). Macpherson was investigating the relationship between Freemasonry and Mozart's *The Magic Flute* when she became seriously ill in early 2012, and she died of cancer on March 21. Jay Macpherson Green now stands at the corner of Macpherson Avenue and Avenue Road in Toronto.

Bibliography

POETRY

Nineteen Poems (Seizin Press, 1952)
O Earth Return (Emblem Books, 1954)
The Boatman (Oxford University Press, 1957)
A Dry Light & The Dark Air (Hawkshead Press, 1959)
The Boatman and Other Poems (Oxford University Press, 1968)
Verse text for 'Jonah—Chamber Cantata for Chorus, Four Soloists,
    and Instruments' by John Beckwith (BMI Canada, 1969)
Welcoming Disaster (Saanes Publications, 1974)
Poems Twice Told (Oxford University Press, 1981)
Half of Life: Lyrics by Friedrich Hölderlin (Aliquando Press, 1995)

PROSE

'Report on the Poetry Readings', in *Writing in Canada*
    (ed. George Whalley, Macmillan, 1956)
'Narcissus: Some Uncertain Reflections' (*Alphabet*, 1960)
'Narcissus: Some Uncertain Reflections; or, From "Lycidas" to
    Donovan's Brain' (*Alphabet*, 1961)
Four Ages of Man: The Classical Myths (Macmillan, 1962)
'Autobiography', in *Literary History of Canada* (ed. Carl F. Klinck,
    University of Toronto Press, 1965)
'Ancient Myth in Modern Poetry', in *Myth and Reality in Irish
    Literature* (Wilfrid Laurier University Press, 1977)
The Spirit of Solitude: Conventions and Continuities in Late Romance
    (Yale University Press, 1982)
'Jay Macpherson' (*University of Toronto Quarterly*, 1992)
'Swift's Very Knowing American' (*Lumen*, 1994)
'Memories of Ottawa' (*Malahat Review*, 1996)
*Biblical and Classical Myths: The Mythological Framework of Western
    Culture* (University of Toronto Press, 2004)
'The Figure of Sarastro: Some Considerations' (*Lumen*, 2006)
'*The Magic Flute* and Freemasonry' (*University of Toronto Quarterly*, 2007)
'"An Immensely Happy Time": Robert Graves Remembered
    by Jay Macpherson (1931–2012)' (*Gravesiana*, 2012)

OTHER

Six Toronto Poets (a recording produced by Jay Macpherson, Folkways, 1958)
'Emblem Drawings' for *The Boatman* (*Alphabet*, 1965)